A Dismantle Approach of likes, retweets and forwards

BHAVYA JAIN

First Published in March 2022

ISBN: 978-93-5472-511-1

BLUEROSE PUBLISHERS

www.bluerosepublishers.com

info@bluerosepublishers.com

+91 8882 898 898

Cover Design:

Muskan

Typographic Design:

Pooja Sharma

Distributed by: BlueRose, Amazon, Flipkart

Introduction

It is to be noted that every day, social media sources declare publicly that they maintain privacy, but is it really so? If that is the case, then we may like to know, what is it that made Whatsapp come into personal spaces and upload privacy particulars? And again, if Twitter was so particular about maintaining privacy, and strict compliance with rules and regulations, why do certain accounts provide content that promotes nudity and pornography? And also, why are these active on their platforms?

If these social media handles take the stand that they are interested to make people connected to them, why are there videos of shootouts and murders active on their platform? Why are there graphics containing sexual harassment openly active on their platform? Are these the principal reasons that make people want to connect with them, or is it a means to manipulate them to their social media handles?

This plethora of undesirable content, displayed on any social media content, shows that there is deliberate access provided towards something which promotes violence. When questions are raised about the appropriateness of such content, then all the above examples cited, are justified by their uploaders as being within the domain of freedom. Basically, a platform which calls itself a source of information and is somewhere being used to pacify mankind but is continuously being used for destructive purposes, belies its core justification.

The main draw to these sites is because one turns to them to have easy access to information, but this easy access is now being used for putting out a lot of manipulative information. Also, the access is now away to put up, a lot of manipulative information. Also, while access is being given freely given to the user, there is no entity as such, who can validate that information resource.

Another reason for this mushrooming growth of undesirable content is because people who are in power, or those who can otherwise use this platform to help maintain more availability, have actually started using it for their own purpose of confusing the masses. People among themselves, have lost their own conscientiousness to understand what is correct, and what is otherwise.

Basically, this book will try to bring out certain insights which will help you, the reader, and the users, to understand that the source of information is actually being used as a manipulative tool to increase access to violence and inappropriate public reactions.

A recent incident which comes to mind in this context is the Farmers' Protest in Delhi on 15 August 2021, which resulted in massive traffic disruption, skirmishes with farmers, and the law maintaining authority, not to mention members of the public who were caught in this milieu. The true facts of this incident were hard to assess as there were two sets of videos that were posted on the same incident.

In one of these videos, it was clearly visible that farmers were seen removing the National Flag. In another video, it was shown that the farmers did not remove the National Flag, but actually planted another, kept on another flagpole. These two videos clearly brought forth two differing mindsets leaving people confused as to what was the actual truth behind the happenings.

The second incident that was brought into the public domain concerned the Congress Party when they decided to hire five lakh social media personnel to work in their social media cell to counter the official handle. One can easily be led to ask why a political party would hire the services of such a large team of content writers for their party and who they euphemistically dubbed 'social media warriors'.

Reverting once again to the ongoing Farmers' Protest on the outskirts of the capital, it is to be noted that the protest had garnered support from a large battery of Hollywood celebrities, such as Mia Khalifa, the American media personality and webcam model, and a former pornographic actress. Surely, the link between her interest in the Indian Farmers' cause and her own area of interest seems to be at cross purposes. Also, the pop star Rihanna was also reported to be siding with the farmers in this protest. Last but not least there was Greta Thunberg, the climate change activist, who, one heard, had not even a passing engagement with the actual cause of the Framer protest in India.

In fact, all these western media celebrities, I am led to conclude, had begun talking and airing their opinion about this issue through their social media handles, without knowing about the issue. I am led to believe that their concern was actually to garner support followed by a tweeter, perhaps a planned social media campaign run by them, in order to degrade a country's image before the world at large.

Thus, there are ample incidents in different countries, of this nature. Why I wonder, the same lot, who were so active in campaigning the Indian Farmers' cause, did not raise their concerns against racism practiced against the Blacks in America or the Visa issue which tried to help American workers to obtain jobs which were being manned by highly skilled Indian trained personnel. But these were never a part of the agenda for the above celebrities. Incidentally, it is also noteworthy to mention that no Indian celebrity came forward to take up the cause of these farmers.

It is clearly evident through this support mechanism of the so-called sympathetic brigade for the Farmers' Cause, that their tweets, which were initially not edited and which clearly showed that one had copied it and floated it, for wider publicity, were there for sinister purposes. It clearly aimed not at garnering sympathy for Farmer issues but for building a campaign against us. Thus, when people questioned these dubious support tweets, such tweets were systematically removed from the Twitter platform promptly.

Coming now to the issue of women's safety, one must examine content presented by teenage girls promoting more of nudity, under the guise of women's empowerment, with hashtags being used. Such content, is actually against privacy policy, in social media. Then why is it on this platform? The concern has become so widespread that even putting power display pictures can be dangerous, since people can start floating information on power point, or just for the 'heck of it'. When such incidents have been reported multiple times, why is it that the social media platform has failed to pull it down?

We are aware that in this generation, users are growing and hence concerns regarding privacy on such platforms should be managed properly. The present status is not just impacting social media but also the lives of people and thereby hampering the fact which actually should be in the limelight.

Contents

Chapter 1

Deep Indoctrination and its Fallout

It is a common saying that we need to dig more, to unearth and understand what at first sight, seems so obvious. This saying is especially relevant when it comes to social media, as social media nowadays has a lot of influencers in the market. Also, in recent times, there is an upsurge of the brainwashing strategies which are being used to influence our generation. Thus, it is important to examine the deep indoctrination of social media and its influences, on the users, in order to understand the reality.

It is therefore a wise standpoint to start this understanding of how social media is an important influencer, by using a simple example. Earlier, this platform was being used exclusively, to promote more talent which was hidden and non-accessible to our belief, because of the boundaries surrounding them. But today, in the light of present-day circumstances, on this platform, the talent being promoted is of a very low standard, while genuine talent is being hidden.

A small child, who randomly sings some lyrics and jingles of a hit song, on a public platform, or social media, is uplifted to such heights of fame that he gets offers of luxury cars and cash as well. Such talent promotion is sheer publicity at all costs and therefore, strikes a death blow for genuine aptitude and genius.

The question arises: Is this really a talent-oriented search on social media platforms? Is it that good to deserve the kind of promotion it is given? We have an ample number of new voices in the singing world, or for that matter in any public sphere, who have the capacity to sing or perform far better, but are still struggling to find their space in the milieu. Their talent is being ignored solely due to social media manipulations.

This situation could have been avoided if social media had, at the outset, created certain rules which could probably hide such undeserving content and promote genuine and better content. That system would actually bring about a better platform for people who really have dedication towards their work.

Another anomaly that is seen on social media is that before showing content which is directed towards the 18+ group, it pops up with the question: 'Are you 18+?' In the same way, can it not pop up with similar queries which will allow better content to be presented on its platform? Since it is an open space, people have started misusing it to seek the limelight and thus present matter which is subconsciously influencing our generation and exposing them to substandard content.

Now let us come to those accounts that have the maximum number of followers. Is it not that the maximum number of followers we have is for Bollywood celebrities, Instagram influencers, and politicians? You might not find the same number of followers on accounts of the Indian Army, the Indian Navy, or even the Indian Air Force. Hence the question arises: To what kind of content are our current generations being driven? Who has the maximum number of followers? Can we use the reach of these accountholders in order to promote digital transformation? But they are actually promoting fake influencers in this digital destruction. The more of fake news they spread and intrusive statements they make, the more they influence the perceptions and attitudes of people. Should 'social media' as the word says, be just used for being 'social'? The generated content presented by influencers supposedly influences them more towards better work. But on closer scrutiny, it is found that it is actually becoming a brainwashing strategy to hamper the mindset of people.

Let us come back to the place we started out, the Farmers' Protest. It was being influenced by those celebrities who didn't even know what exactly is happening in the system. Yet. they were passing statements which were triggering off people to stand up against what they wanted to present in the public domain.

The answer to this state of affairs is very clear. These posts and statements were coming from their respective teams, which is in the public domain. Let us take another example...the Jawaharlal Nehru University case, where celebrities like Farhan Khan and Deepika Padukone came forward to take a stand. When one news channel asked them: 'Why are you here?' their reply was: 'Since there are a lot many people speaking against the system, probably there is something wrong.'

So, a celebrity who does not even know what is happening on the ground level comes up in the mob to take a stand with the students. They were the ones who do not know the core realities of the situation. Hence, what was the logic behind their coming to this scenario? The answer is simple. Their PR teams work to find places where they can seek the limelight. Later on, after the damage is done, the check is undertaken as to whether their support was genuine, or not. It was later revealed that all these things were actually found to be paid promotions.

So, today's social media consumer gulps what he sees in the very first place. Therefore, the onus of responsibility falls on social media to find a strategy to sift and understand what is important and what is otherwise, and what should be engaging for the consumer.

Hence, the fact that social media is proactively growing, there is a need to draw a line and present what is authentic and disallow what is not.

Chapter 2

A Down, Right Thumb on Social Media

As the latest trend happening on social media, be it on Twitter, Facebook, Instagram, etc. the upright thumb is actually making the consumer unproductive and in consequence, more anti-social. As it rightly professes, the social media platform gives us a larger platform to reach people and to interact with a larger set of audiences. But the current hashtag trend is actually making the younger generation focus on the limelight and on content which more than anything, turns them into look-alike morons, as the content they are drawn to, is not useful.

Among the general public it is noticed that in order to gain more attention, people have started to copycat what celebrities are doing on their accounts. This leads me to query: 'Have we just forgotten the ways to our intelligence?' The reason why I am led to this query is because whether it be a five-year-old child or a 50-year-old adult, in order to catch attention on themselves, they have started creating content which does not seem to make any sense. It seems that this increased connectivity has made us stupid, rather than being smart.

In order to please the audience, the younger generation spends an ample amount of hours in clicking pictures, to grab the attention for themselves and their activities. The question thus arises: Why are we so addicted? Why are we turning so narcissistic? Social media was apparently meant to be 'social' but evidently, it has turned both children and adults into users who use their tools to dedicate and misspend the right amount of time in engaging with content which should not even be present on the platform. According to recent research, it has been seen that if you are not giving at least four to five hours to social media, as an individual, then you start feeling socially isolated.

So, be it a politician or a celebrity, we hardly ever know what is happening in their real lives, but thanks to their Public Relations (PR) team, and the content presented by them, every common person feels an affinity with these people who are in the limelight, and begin to suppose that they are living a happy life. Subsequently, in order to find the same happiness, every next individual has started imitating them. These snare tools have actually started working as dopamine to experience the pleasure of being alive. They all run to platforms like Tik Tok and Instagram reels for this image retrieval exercise.

People have started creating content to find the same aspects which the celebrities are living. They do not stop to ponder and think that if this was the real picture of our celebrities' or politicians' lifestyle, why do we have those views about actors and actresses committing suicide? Are we really forgetting that all these people who are in the limelight are there because of the attention to them given by us? If we, as the audience take our support away from them, they will be exactly like us, living a common life. Since we have started posting only their admirable and coveted aspects, on different platforms, people feel conscious about expressing their dark side.

To get an ample number of likes and love reactions on social media, today's generation has just forgotten a simple picture of real life. Scrolling through different pages to different reels and from posting their own vacation pictures, and party nights, we have just forgotten to appreciate a simple life. While browsing through different platforms we tend to find content that has the maximum number of views and so feel that if we also present the same content, on those very platforms, people will find us more in the limelight.

I had wished that during the Pandemic also when the world was being asked to sit back at home, our dear celebrities would follow the rules, Instead, they decided to go for vacations, due to which, a certain set of people forgot the dangerous impact of the disease. To imitate exactly just what their favorite stars were doing, they started risking their own lives. This leads me to conclude that it's necessary to even have the 'Down Right Thumb' sign to let them know that not every content that is presented by them, is admirable and worth imitating.

Not just the celebrities, our dearest politicians too, in order to amplify their work, have their personal photographers and media coverage people assigned. So even in their post, where the room they are posing in, is seemingly clean, the politician is seen holding a broom in his or her hand, to give off the feeling that the room has been cleaned by them only. What the ground reality is, we are not likely to find out, but what is presented on the social media platform, is what we are led to believe in blindly, and so condescend to undergo a leap as per the content.

Hence, these platforms are not tarnishing our conscious mind but are also making us internet troll material. The fear of missing out has made us a 'FOMO' generation, through direct representation into social media circles. So apparently, we are 'drugged' into believing what social media is showing, where everyone is living a happy life and all the negative feelings and emotions have gone to another planet.

Furthermore, we're not allowed to get depressed because we have to portray the perfect man to the world. We are running a rat race to please the world and, in the bargain, forgetting the negative patterns of life too. I wish social media would provide a length of the proverbial rope by means of which we can identify the distorted reality of these people in the limelight. After all, not every printer is required to depict the dark spots of life, and not every upright thumb is required to like the feedback presented by the people.

Chapter 3

The Forward Label

Who knew in the year 2007 that a social media platform which was meant merely to send messaging services frequently, would become a reason for creating violence? The social media messaging service WhatsApp, which is being spoken about here is one that states that they provide end-to-end encryption which allows the consumer to view messages only which are stored in their device. By that logic, it thus allows you to maintain your privacy.

Hence on paper, WhatsApp appears to be a secure instant messaging platform. But one is faced with the query arising thereof: If they are providing end-to-end encryption, then WhatsApp has to come to everyone's personal space to justify that they are maintaining privacy! If they are actually providing end-to-end encryption then how come WhatsApp was able to keep its status in each user?

So, the question arises: Are they really maintaining the privacy they claim to maintain? Today, this social media platform has more than one billion users across the globe. This achievement has made this platform become significant now, at creating emotional targeting, through its forwards.

In order to curb the violence created by forwards, WhatsApp identified the frequently forwarded messages with a double arrow icon. It actually decided to limit the number of people to 256 in each group. Seemingly effective, on closer examination, one realizes that the system is fraught with flaws.

The question arises: Does limiting to 256 people actually make sense? Presumably, it may be argued that these 256 members together might share the same kind of opinion, or taste for a particular topic and these 256 members individually are facilitating the spread of their opinion to other 256 members in another group. So, with using simple logic one can conclude that creating a boundary around 256 members does not seem to make sense. These groups are dynamically increasing and their agenda is being well forwarded to others.

So, to restrict these 256 members from spreading their opinion to the rest of the people WhatsApp created one more boundary. It was stated that these 256 members in the group would share their opinion with only five people in the group. By that arithmetic, if one person is forwarding one message to five people or groups, the same cycle is repeated by the receiver. Do we really need to multiply and explain a message to five people or groups? It does not seem to make sense.

So, what exactly are these rules doing? Are they created to curb the spread of violence created by manipulating the forward label? To check the ground reality, we have to recall the example of rampant abuse that was present after the application of these rules. It was found that in India itself, around 18-25 cases of child abuse, kidnapping, lynching was witnessed.

Even the media report stated that the stringer attached is still not in control. A case in point that may well be recalled is the instance in which school children who were in a group were found guilty of harassing a schoolgirl in the group Later, it was proven that it was a mock attempt of girls in a group to prove that they were being harassed.

Such cases have not been stopped yet, On the contrary, they are seen to be increasing in number. This is just at a mediocre level. We have our dearest known figures who too, have been found by reliable sources to be involved with drug peddlers, in a social media group of this kind.

Now the scenario is that because of such apps happening, even the police, who were on the streets just to check traffic violations and verify driving licenses, is now being dragged into checking WhatsApp chats to find out which people are involved in the buying and selling of such contraband material. We really don't need to come up with their names or tell you the stories of persons who have been involved in such acts.

Not just drug cases but even the most horrifying terrorist attacks are being well planned in these groups.

So, what exactly is the position taken by these WhatsApp calls as regards the regulation of privacy protection and the controlling of such acts? It must be noted that people tend to believe such dangerous misinformation. They are still continuously forwarding them to people. The irony is that even to get the Almighty's blessings, nowadays the consumer finds himself connected with the next ten people who too, are desirous of receiving a fruitful result!

From getting good morning messages to getting ways on how to wear your undergarments, WhatsApp has truly proved that it is an elite manipulative platform. The viral content is continuously promoting fake information and rumors and people are failing to understand the truth. God knows what is not working right and leading to this runaway proliferation for WhatsApp. Is it the consumer failing to find the right to people, or is it the multiplier factor which WhatsApp potentially thinks is a subtraction factor?

In the latter case then do we need to help them understand the basic difference between multiplication and subtraction? Do we need to explain to ourselves as to which of the Almighty's messages should be forwarded to the next ten people?

Chapter 4

The Hyper curated Posts

Have you read recently of how a model posed near her dead father's coffin? By doing so, the model glamorized her late father's death spot with a photoshoot. Not just that... there was another influencer who trampled on the plants in a conservatory despite the staff repeatedly asking her to refrain from stepping on their precious plantings. Elsewhere, a Yoga instructor stepped into a coffin to pose her Yoga look.

This whole trend of getting engagement with a certain type of community has brought the level of empathy down, as also an increase in hyper-curated posts. As far as I remember, the vision created hashtags on Instagram, of photos, states that your mobile photos will not be mediocre with them. 'Our awesome filters will transform mobile photos into a professional look', is their promise.

By the same logic, therefore, this photo and video sharing platform, therefore, was intended to create videos and photos with a professional look so that both the individual and the brand connect with their audience uniquely. TODAY, this, 500 million strong user, platform has the highest engagement platform with its audience through exposure presented by the influencers.

In order to gain active engagement with impressions, and a higher level of tax, it seems these influencers have lost their common sense. As far as I can recall, these influencers were present in the market to build a relationship with the customers through their posts. Keeping the traditional approach of marketing, these posts of the influencers were used to drive more audience towards the product.

But currently, it seems that these influencers in order to gain a certain amount of money have loaded the platform with their vain posts. Nowadays the whole Instagram feed consists of nothing but revealing, unrealistic standards of beauty. Hence, to gain some amount of love reacts to their post, these influencers, who are responsible for creating progress in digital content, are actually inspiring unrealistically, the temptation to get hyper-curated looks

The question thus arises: What is making such influencers more ... in the market? In order to understand this phenomenon I decided to explore the accounts of this platform and came across an estimate which suggested that even if you have more than 1000 followers, you can easily engage your audience . What I realized thereof is that this Instagram model is basically more for creating money through their posts.

The revealing finding led me to believe that the formula is as simple as one that states that if you have more followers, plus more likes on your posts, you can easily mint money out of it. Many influencers, (and perhaps you will not be inclined to resort to this), are making money while sharing their revealing picture as in the market. Thus, we don't really need to explain why the engagement for such posts is so high.

If we have to look at the percentage of users of Instagram, then it will be seen that people of the age group of 19-25 are around 32%, whereas in the age group of 35-45 it is around 40%and 50% of users are female. We see that this platform has the maximum engagement with teenagers and adults, for it. This image-centric social media platform is actually creating a disillusion about life, in the market In order to gain attention to itself, not just revealing posts but also glamorous proposals are also making the simple way of living difficult.

Apart from these glamorous posts the engagement of this whole Instagram community has made teenagers vulnerable and has created an artificial presentation of all life and interaction therein. All the above-mentioned incidents reiterate that we have lost a sense of reality and a loss of empathy towards life. The real story has got hidden somewhere in the background, under the superficial veil.

I'm not sure if I should lay the blame solely on this social media platform, or should lay some of the blame on the lack of common sense of these influencers. This is because Instagram never stated that such content would help one to earn money. The motive was simple: to create brands through your post to drive audiences towards your community. Thus, the way this generation is getting influenced by these so-called influencers is not the same as what would have been contributed, had they used their brains and rejected such comments and opted for less interaction. In that case, Instagram would probably not have been overcrowded with such derogatory content.

Besides all these superfluous posts, we have accounts even on Instagram which are continuously mocking the gods of a particular religion. In spite of reporting them hundreds of times, there is no such barrier insight that stops such users from creating such objectionable content on its platform. A recent incident reiterating this fact is one wherein a Delhi resident had filed a complaint against the platform for showing Lord Shiva in an objectionable manner. The sole intention we all know was to incite the followers and promote hatred and disharmony.

The complaint was demanded and a criminal act was filed against the CEO of Instagram and other authorities, under Sec153 and 259A of the Indian Penal Code and sections of the IPC Act. But despite taking this incident to that level, Instagram continues to have content creators who promote Hindu phobic videos and posts.

Now this situation deems that I ask: Like the other platform is Instagram too, avoiding such acts and finds itself cool with such content? It's easier for Instagram when such content presented leads towards taking action on other communities, but not when it is a part of one particular community.

Recently, an Instagram influencer posted a statement that all the Jain monolithic statues are promoting nudity. Thus, I would ask the same group: If these monolithic figures are promoting nudity, then what about porn stars who are keeping their revealing posts on the platform? Are they promoting content which promotes nudity or vice versa of the nudity? It is easier to pass such statements, but I guess these influencers have forgotten that there are religious sentiments attached to these figures by some people. It is considered justifiable to condemn something if you don't believe in it, but it is not necessary that what you believe is appropriate, or is universally applicable.

As an influencer, you are responsible for driving engagement with your posts but not imposing your thoughts in your followers' minds. Yet initially, I felt that it is only these insane people who are responsible for such contradictions, but now when I see this whole platform promoting such people altogether, it shows a clear indication that only a few love reactions are not responsible. Actions are not just required against such unskilled people but also against the platform which is openly working with such content creators.

Chapter 5

Retweets Not Equal to Endorsements

That little blue bird came up on the social media platform to speak in multiple voices initially in 140 words. But today, it seems the bird was unhappy to stand in with just 140 words!

Initially, this bird welcomed all kinds of voices, but as time had passed, this sweet little bird has created its own library of playlists. The question thus arises: How come this bird got its runaway attention in the past five years?

Way back in 2006, when this sweet little bird came into the picture it had few users, who would listen to the 'lyrics' of certain users. Likewise, when this sweet little bird came into India, Thirumalai Velu was the first person who created an Indian voice on this platform. This bird struggled to create its presence among her peers such as Facebook and WhatsApp, who both had crossed their kindergarten days among their users, whereas this bluebird was learning how to baby walk among the seniors.

Today, the question(revelation) is that most of the people on this platform, are performing actors across the globe, whereas the other two platforms, who initially were good with their progress, are today just left out where this brand forges ahead with blank DPs and copied status. Today, if we want to know any major thing or even the slightest change, then Twitter, through its auto-refreshing updates will let you know what is happening around, every second, with its trending Hashtags, be it News, Sports, or Entertainment, you can quickly know what is happening around.

It is rightly said that when too much attention is given to something, it makes it over pampered and transforms it into a limelight seeker. This bird today is the star among its peers and is the reason why every person on this platform is creating its voice through the power of public conversation.

I remember once when I was traveling by train, there were certain issues I felt, as a passenger, and I kept the same information about my problem on this platform. At the very next stop, action was taken against the same. It was there that I realized that this platform has a lot of potential to reach every single authority easily. I guess the reason why "Maseeha" of Bollywood became famous.

While Maseeha was helping the common man during the Pandemic, nobody questioned the fact that from which source this film was privy to so many resources. While the public started praising him for his efforts, during the Pandemic, using Twitter, I sat there clueless, thinking if somebody had so much money and resources why did the concerned person not utilize these funds for his own career? But thanks to Twitter marketing which had created demi-gods on this planet.

But unfortunately, the same Maseeha was accused of a 20-crore cash evading scandal. Oh! I think my first question there itself, was correct, as to how did Maseeha have so many resources? I guess it was this unexplained fact that led to his coming under the scanner.

The same question came to my mind during the Farmers' Protest, when I spotted Rihanna's tweet for the Farmers' Protest when she questioned why we Indians, were not talking about this. I sat there thinking as to why she was talking about this matter. I guess it was because a population of 138 crore Indians had already indulged themselves enough, in thinking about what was happening in their own nation.

But then, how come this lady from Bridgetown got so nervous about the situation here? Did she even know from where these people (so-called farmers) were coming? Did she even know the place to which they belonged? I guess the answer to all these questions is a 'No'. Then, one wonders, why exactly Robyn Rihanna Fenty was concerned about the Farmers' Protest.

This simple tweet of her questioning the situation in our country was surely not out of her concern for the Indian farmers. She was actually paid 2.5 million dollars for this question. No matter what the PR Team says, we all know with legitimate proof to back this revelation, which was later deleted from the platform, that her tweet had Khalistan links.

There are an ample number of other issues which require global attention but this tweet was a sure disingenuous attempt to bring our nation into a bad light. All the top Bollywood celebrities too were supporting her. Very few came up and stated that this situation is our internal matter.

The same set of above-mentioned tweets from this source werebeing seen from a porn star to an environmentalist. Everyone was talking about it as if it was an Indian movie that had won an Oscar for its effort. Oops! I just remembered that Oscars are only awarded to Indian movies when you present India in crises, or below the poverty line!

Coming back to the tweets trend, over the past two years, many campaigns were drawn on this platform. Not just Bollywood celebrities but also organizations like PETA were also highly active at giving reverse feeds to the public. Many of the accounts on this platform were even blocked when they put too many uncomfortable questions to such organizations.

I recall that when Bollywood celebrities and sportspersons came upon this platform to provide their knowledge on Hindu festivals, a few users when they had questioned the same people on other communities' festivals, many of their accounts were being locked. PETA India too outwardly kept a message for all the users who questioned them on their silence on a particular community's festivals. This same organization, that does not find milk to be a vegan diet item, remains silent when questioned on the killing of an animal at a particular festival.

I must say not just the real picture of these people and organisations have come into the limelight but the reverse too, has surfaced. One must concede that there are a certain set of users who have used this platform properly to question them. But all these trending hashtags which have been used to deteriorate our country's image have also been used to create certain irrational logic and this platform has given a lot of space to such negative statements.

As I have said earlier, this bird which was once struggling to create its space has today dynamically changed itself by giving power to such unnecessary logic. What's wrong if the government decided to keep an eye on all these digital platforms when stand-up comedians used the same platform to Twitter about their own country and its culture in the name of freedom of speech? It is highly justifiable, therefore, in the light of the above-mentioned situation, for the government to keep an eye on these platforms.

It is important to demarcate a clear difference between a vogue of profanity and the real picture. There are an ample number of instances which can be shared to speak more about businesses running on these platforms, but for the same, we need to deep dive a bit more to know how things are running, around us. And before I take you to the real picture of these platforms how about you, my reader, doing your bit, by reporting such accounts that propagate vague statements against our nation? In case you do so, you will find that your own account would get suspended! So, try it at your own risk.

Chapter 6

The Focal Engagement

Till now, I have given ample examples of instances where a consumer has been interacting with brands, on different social media platforms. Also, I have pointed out instances of how a customer is trying to get information about a particular topic and how a consumer is communicating the same information to other people.

As a follow-through, my question to you is, after understanding the whole engagement of social media and the consumer, would you be in a position to tell me what is being affected the most? Is it a consumer cognitive engagement, or is it a behavioral engagement between the two? Is it more of a positive influence, or is it?

more on the negative side? I am led to feel that after reading about the last few scenarios, you might be under the impression that what is being affected is negative.

But right now, I would like to flip the coin and show you a whole community engagement. At the outset, I must apprise you that this is not an attempt to start a marketing chapter for you. The purpose of it is far removed from any such cognizance. It is more like connecting the dots which are scattered far behind. Recently, on Women's Day, Mcdonalds' reversed its letter to 'MW' as an attempt to show their love and affection towards womenfolk, on Women's Day. Also, several local brands too, promoted their business through these platforms, thereby making locals more vocal. The exercise resulted in not just an increase in market reach, but also a means of getting international reach.

While on the other hand, we must acknowledge that around 80% of all these platforms have been misused, at least 20% of them are still bringing positive outcomes for a whole online community. I, therefore, field a guess that this is the reason why every second person is on social media.

From brand trust to brand loyalty, every local product is now on social media. This new phase is more like a conceptual model where an online interaction of an individual towards a brand engagement is bringing out more product involvement.

But again I come back to the other side of the coin where the credibility of these platforms is poor. One is led to surmise that this dismal record is the reason behind their dismal approach of likes and Retweets and forwards, which is hidden! Over the last eight years, I have been like a 600m runner for all these platforms. The reason is that if we do a tantamount analysis, of their videos and the photos, they tend to have differing impacts on a consumer's mind.

Embedded YouTube videos, in contrast with Instagram and Facebook posts that stimulated impacts, are different. In their case, it is more like a game-related approach, where the minds of people are being played with and manipulated, via this gaming strategy.

To reiterate my point of view, I am tempted to request you to tell me, what you recall absorbing, the first time you saw a post on Instagram or Facebook, or when you saw a video by them. The cognitive approach is that your mind absorbs the whole information and then the behavioral adjustments towards it, starts reacting

I guess that is the reason why the information which has been shared in the last few chapters is more on the platform. If we take this, the user-generated matrix, and classify into audience growth and monetary benefit, you will find that all these platforms have a win-win situation on both the poles.

The factors which are influencing more such negative content are quite high. This is the reason why, be it a common man or a pop star, everyone has fallen into the trap of growth and monetary benefits. I'm sure while reading this, you can yourself surmise why people are rushing towards online marketing platforms.

Incidentally, we don't have a scrutinizing technique that can classify what is good from what is bad. Currently, the best comparison would be that it is more like mixing a batter that has a lot of salt and just a pinch of sugar!

Chapter 7

A Horror Movie

Way back in 2016, Founder and CEO) of Facebook, Mark Zuckerberg, in a full-page advertisement wrote: "We have a responsibility to protect your data, and if we can't then we don't deserve to serve you."

This happened when Facebook came into the limelight after its data privacy scandal.

Coincidentally, it seems, inspired by the same advertisement even the Delhi Chief Minister kept a pull page advertisement on the subject of 'Making Delhi Cleaner'. It seems that both these authorities react on a similar circuit, after being caught in a huge court scandal. Their actions seem to be on the lines of the proverbial saying, about thieves, where they were confessing to saying: 'We have not committed the theft.'

The rising scandals of these social media platforms show a track record of situations which highlight insufficient measures are taken for data privacy. If you joggle your mind you are bound to remember such occurrences. An instance of this data privacy scandal revolved around the capturing of the personal information of up to 87 million people by a political consulting firm Cambridge Analytica. The firm was able to capture the maximum information of the user through a personality with App called: 'This is your life'.

The information gathered by the firm was quite useful in building up an entire range of psychographic profiles of the users. Even the researchers stated that this information could be used to predict highly sensitive personal attributes of the users. Be its personality traits, political views, or religious views, this whole model is lucrative for social media platforms to mint money.

Let us understand how: When you create a Facebook profile, you add your basic information, which is then reflected on the platform. This includes your name, your gender, added to your interests. Your gender too is vital information for the platform. Even when you try to hide it, your area of interest on the platform will be a giveaway and will help the social media platform to predict it easily.

So even if you write that you are a male, but choose to like up pages or accounts connected to gay groups the platform itself, in spite of you hiding facts, will label you as gay. So, what you might be saying in an attempt to fool the platform would turn around and actually become the platform which is fooling you. This cheat sheet created by the platform is basically exposed to numerous vital information.

In 2016, when the USA election campaigns were happening, it has been alleged that a Canadian political data firm, called 'Aggregate IQ', was exposed to micro-targeting tools that influenced voters throughout the campaign. It has been also stated that this information database was being collectively used to target individuals, using various methods. Now, this included Facebook and political websites, hashtags and even emails.

All these internal experiments till now show how these platforms breach the trust. I'm sure a few months back you had seen that Facebook had acquired multiple Apps. It is thus being stated now that Facebook owns everything! since Instagram too, was being acquired, as also WhatsApp, Oculus, Life rein. Threadsy, ... you name it and you'll discover that Facebook has acquired the same.

Just give a thought to this phenomenon. What is it that makes Facebook acquire all these top companies? The answer is a simple one. All these platforms will provide Facebook with information which is vital for Facebook, ranging from emotional detection Apps to face recognition App, and it is Facebook that owns it.

The conclusion you can safely decipher is that it is not just Google but even Facebook that has entered into our spaces. Earlier, people were wrangling over the fact that Google had every information of the individual, but my dear friend, we ourselves have given our information to even Facebook now.

Even if this state of affairs does not ring alarm bells, then let me apprise you about a recent allegation that came into the forefront, wherein a former Facebook communication official stated that the company kept profits a priority over and above its enforcement against hate speech and misinformation. They even went on to say that this developed App is just a namesake social media platform which connects people.

It is apparent that their goal is simple. It is oriented towards penetrating into that segment of the market which is even untapped by Google and thereby become the sole source of information. Does it not give you goosebumps to realise how easily, and without even the effort of marketing themselves, they have occupied our spaces?

On an off chance, did you even know how this situation had come to pass? When Google was demanding of its CEO Sundar Pichai the stopping the protecting of the harassment clause, Facebook took advantage of this information and decided to build an empire for itself, even bypassing Google, the erstwhile and sole source of the importance of safety in the work environment. In an interview, an ex-Google engineer stated that she was being forced to have one-on-one sessions with the harassers and was not even allowed to express her discomfort.

While Google was and is still trying to hide such sexual harassment cases, Facebook as a social media platform slowly has occupied and has taken all possible measures to be the next Google so that the next time when you want to make a search you directly land up on Facebook.

The manner in which they have acquired the above-mentioned Apps, even they were not able to grab information from your favourite influencers and popular Instagram accounts and are using to promote more misinformation

This whole information was being collected by the social media focused marketing company 'Chtrbox'. They were also able to gain access to a number of followers, profile pictures, and private contacts information. So, while you continue your preparation of creating the not-so-beautiful but actually distressing videos to please your audience, all these social media platforms, with a bucket of popcorn, are sitting back and watching a blockbuster movie where we are all morons dancing and even paying them to watch us!

Chapter 8

All Over in the Blink of an Eye

It is better to overlook than to overwrite. I guess that is the reason why both Google and Facebook re-branded themselves. In 2015, that time, Google did its corporate restructuring into a parent company called, 'Alphabet Inc.' and it seemed that Facebook on 28 October 2021, even changed the logo outside its building!

Following these moves, the question arises as to why these brands are doing so. To understand this, we need to understand what exactly leads to corporate restructuring. The major reasons which have been observed behind this step have been brought upon if the management is struggling in its efficiency, or when the company is into economic loss, or if the organization is failing to keep its assets working well. In the current case, all these factors were actually influencing both the companies and so it was important for them to have a brand revival.

In 2015, when Google was changing its operations, it was important for Google to resort to such a step so that it could divert all attention from the ongoing cases of sexual harassment happening, spyware attacks, and abuses on the workers of the company.

All this sudden shift actually helped Google to take its time out for finding ways to hide the major concerns and to show that Google is not evil. Today, Zuckerberg has taken exactly the same step when the controversy of leaking information came into the picture. As Zuckerberg said: 'Meta Platforms Inc in the future would be helpful for people to teleport instantly as a hologram at the office, without a commute.' But it is in the 'future' only, not now.

The question, therefore, arises, when it is for the future, why has it been unveiled by the company now? The answer to the same is simple. 'Meta Platforms Inc doesn't want to be only a social media platform. It is going to position itself in such a manner that all the consumers will, by their own volition, become prisoners of this platform. The future would thus lead to this question: 'Why Google when Meta Platforms Inc is here?' Facebook has hugely invested in augmented reality. Not just the oculus glasses but there is much more in this business.

In all-pervasive situations, this virtual reality would play an important role in our lives. This one step has been used to shift the tension from the political battles and bad press which Facebook is fighting right now.

Chapter 9

Not so Private

In a recent article published by 'India Today', it has been stated that we can report abuses and offensive WhatsApp messages, to the Department of Telecommunications. As far as I remember, it has also been stated that we have an option to flag offensive messages as 'improper' on WhatsApp. The question that arises is, how this can be possible if the message provider states that they offer end-to-end encryption. Hence the above claim by WhatsApp is automatically contradicted by WhatsApp itself

If you are reviewing the improper messages then how does the end-to-end encryption fit into the scheme of things? The simple fact behind Facebook-owned ...App is that Facebook employs about 900 WhatsApp reviewers whose entire job is to check these offensive messages planted by us. So there is nothing private. It is obvious that the proverbial 'Godrej Lock' can be broken by the thief!

It seems that these security cases who apparently say we are secure, have given the passwords to the thief to open messages easily. So now, before you think of making payments and through the WhatsApp services which have been recently introduced, think about what information, via these transactions, you are sharing with them. Basically, WhatsApp is misleading its two billion users. The things on which they pride themselves are more on humility.

So let us understand what exactly we are sharing with WhatsApp. I guess it was only yesterday that you were chatting with some friend about a break-up, wherein she shared the screenshots of her messages with her 'Ex'. In those messages, you can see that her 'Ex' even asked her to buy him a new cell phone. So dear reader, you tell me, what is the nature of the information that we users, inadvertently, might have shared with WhatsApp?

Or wait! Before your friend defends herself saying that she has cleaned her device and removed all the chat with him, and also deleted the screenshots of the same, don't come up with the statement that WhatsApp was being bluffed., just because the things have vanished.

Let me tell you that WhatsApp can easily access this chat and the screenshots of the same. Let me tell you that be it Apple, Google, or both of them, they can access WhatsApp Cloud back-ups and so, even the so-called 'private' messaging service provider warns its users to ensure that such backups fall outside its end-to-end encryption.

So, my dear reader, your friend has not bluffed the service provider at all, but actually, it is a friend who is waylaid into a trap. WhatsApp will restore all the messages on a clean device by just using mobile numbers. Hence, your friend has not just entertained her 'Ex' but also the service provider employed too.

It seems to be fun for the company employees. Every day they are finding new stories which are not just spicy but have a lot many emotions involved in them. Do you not recall how even as kids, we would hear new stories from our grandparents? It seems in the 21st Century we are the 'grandparents' for the service provider. Even WhatsApp's rival 'Telegram App' claims to have come with the same allegations, warning that there is a fault in this end-to-end encryption.

Now the next question that arises is, that if there is a community to review improper messages then how is it that the maximum number of forwarded messages regarding terrorist attacks, political views, which apparently lead to violence, harassment, or sexual exploitation messages, are even existing in the ecosystem. Is the public failing to understand which content sent on a recipient device is positive and which of them is negative? Such instances we have already seen have been varying political fights, and even terrorist attacks have been planned on WhatsApp groups.

It seems that just to remain the Number One service provider they have opened their doors to everyone. Also, their so-called standards of security are quite confusing. In today's technology, we do have automated translation tools which can help to differentiate and assess what is real and what is fake. Then one may wonder how it is that in a recent instance a couple of months ago, during the fight between the Left and Right-Wingers of Brazil and Mexico, even after banning of these groups, which were sending problematic messages, there were still thousands of such messages floating. Hence, we don't seem to exactly gauge what privacy WhatsApp is talking about.

Chapter 10

A Graffiti of Political Images

There are an ample number of photographs that get viral on Social Media. Recently, a few of them had earned the dubious claim of showing a lot of misinformation. It seems we have many photoshop experts around. One of them recently created a post wherein it showed the Honorable Prime Minister being abused at a rally. Later on, the same post was claimed to be false.

There was another post by a Twitter user which claimed that the Congress Party was using the image of the same elderly for all its rallies. The post stated that Congress Party had paid the elderly woman Rs 5000/ for all the photoshoots. The same post was later deleted by the user.

It has also been stated that the Congress Party's IT cell had photoshopped an image wherein there was a comparison being shown between Prime Minister Modi and Adolph Hitler. The said image had been circulated both on Facebook and Twitter. Later on, the post was picked up for clarification by all news channels, by stating that the said post was being deliberately created.

The reason behind bringing up all these scenarios is to clearly indicate that currently, Social Media is increasingly being used mostly to influence political information. Earlier, and before 2014, figures and statistics show that Social Media never had such a widespread impact on Indian politics.

To understand how effectively Social Media is helping the political parties in amplifying their information, let us assess the timeline since when Social Media has become the game-changer in Indian politics. Prior to this rise, for conventional mass communication, you may recall, our politicians used to do campaigns and rallies and even visited rural areas to harness their attempt to reach their voters.

Gone are the days when, due to these campaigns, which were majorly street movements, life in cities came to a standstill, and we school goers, used to get holidays. Today, politicians make 'movements' on social media. All this changeover effectively started in 2012, when in that year, social activist Anna Hazare used Social Media for his anti-corruption movement to interact with the people of New Delhi. This one movement we all remember and realise was massively being spread through social media.

It seems BJP during the General Elections in 2014, understood the technique of how to gather votes from its voters. So, a month before the start of the General Elections I remember the title adopted by Prime Minister Modi on Twitter and Instagram, that he had kept was: 'Chowkidar Narendra Modi'. The same title was being used by the Members of the BJP Party and sheer supporters of the party. The Prime Minister and the Party members clearly knew how the campaign was going to gather the attention of consumers., by this move. At the same time, equally aggressively, to defame the party, the Opposition Congress Party, changed the slogan to 'Chowkidar Chor Hai'.

Well, the pun between the Congress Party and the BJP sites have always been the favourites of our Social Media consumers. It seems more of a World Cup match wherein India is fighting against Pakistan. On the other hand, BJP's online campaign in 2014, showed exceptionally satisfactory results. And from that point onwards, Social Media became the game-changer in Indian politics.

The traditional ways of sending promises, which at one time were the passwords of Indian politics, at these elections were not seen much. It has been stated that during this period nearly one-third of first-time voters got influenced through these Social Media campaigns. A report by ADG online states that 30% of the 10 million first-time voters were influenced and were engaging more on Social Media.

So, all these online interactions, trolls, and posts, clearly state that today, to reach either the urban or the rural voters all you have to do is be significantly active on Social Media. After the winning of the BJP in 2014, a maximum number of Maharashtra regional parties became active on Social Media. Recently, BJP leaders who are involved in elections-related publicly to 'Economic Times' that the party's total advertisements expenditure accounted for 20-25% of the total budget and which were posted on these Social Media campaigns. They spent nearly Rs. 37 crores on Facebook advertisements. During the same period in question, the Congress Party had spent Rs. ten lakhs whereas regional parties had spent Rs 20 lakhs.

So Social Media platforms, for whom we were the only source of income, are today, minting money through these political parties' status updates.

Chapter 11

Hashtag

We all know this symbol, which most of us use to see on our landline phones, thinking what is the purpose of the same, when we use to dial numbers, has today, the same symbol, without even keeping the numbers, is marking a conversation on different platforms. This allows not just the building of a trend but also allows quick retrieval of information on any given topic.

For anyone looking for updated news on any event, this hashtag symbol can help them read the information. It thus seems to be the viral sensation on any platform and one finds a need to be exposed more to hashtag activism to assess its onward outreach.

Due to this symbol, even mainstream media has failed to catch the real news. All that these news sources have been piled with, is a mass of hashtags on their platform. This is also the reason why these hashtags have become a sensation in digital activism. So as a recall, remember the hashtag 'Chowkidar' that was altered to 'Chowkidar Chor Hai.' It is thus evident that important campaigns are emerging, due to this symbol.

As it is important to understand and examine how this symbol works, let us understand this situation with the help of a relevant example. Recently, Bollywood actors Vicky Kaushal and Katrina Kaif got married. In order to garner updated news of their wedding events, one used the hashtag 'VickyKat'. This one reference actually worked as a clerical information center wherein you simply kept the hashtag and the system quickly retrieved related information for you.

At the same time, this symbol also worked in a semiotic sense. To understand this, let us take another example. In order to mark something new on the platform, you actually file a new hashtag so that it enables the users to get to know what is new in the information system. This whole system of coding and adding new comments have actually created a framework wherein it has become difficult to assess the real context of Social Media utterance. The real activism has got hidden in this poor hashtag activism. The reason why the 'Me Too' Campaign had not just the real story but also fake events in it, in order to be a part of this growing campaign, Social media influencers had created twisted and manipulated information in the public domain.

This one symbol has now been the main reason to distribute false information and has targeted individual citizens for performing its aggressive operations. It seems to be a chronic disease, wherein we are entrapped with fake information in the system. We have seen multiple incidents wherein Social media writers have created and shared huge amounts of posts that can speculate wars in the future. This time around, this hashtag, without the numbers, is helping you to connect all the wrong numbers of the platform.

Even the rape culture has been seen to systematically increase. Since the influencers, in this case, were actually a web version of opinion, (they were) leaders in the creating and spreading of fake news. I could have even mentioned incidents where information or news regarding any rape incident that has been on the platform is manipulated by Social Media propaganda writers, thereby confusing the audience as to what's the real truth behind the scene.

And the fact that they overlook these incidents is that while creating sensational hashtags concerning the news regarding a raped woman, such incidents are not the masala for audiences. So before one puts one's trust in this fully registered news, on the platforms, it is worthwhile to have a look at an ample number of posts with similar hashtags. You will end up fathoming out the inhuman nature of these influencers who apparently act and cry out for a web-safe environment but actually have made themselves the most unsafe environment on the web. Hence, remember that behind every hashtag is a reliable source that is both influencer and manipulator of the truth.

Chapter 12

The Mirage of Interaction

By this time, and currently, we are clear about the fact that Social Media platforms are not merely facilitating, but are actually shapers of social acts. So, the more you acknowledge, interact, and redistribute through your 'likes', 'shares', and 'mentions', the more you are defining real-life outcomes. This is the reason behind why, if we author on a daily basis, these platforms have become a new ... in the market, for cybercriminals.

Hence, observing the same fact, I tried understanding deeply just what the public is looking for. While understanding the same, I realized that around sixty percent of social media users, turn to these platforms to amplify their self-brand, while the remaining forty percent are unconcerned about public attention. Using the same facts, a number of cases, in areas such as cyberbullying, stalking, sexual harassment, and identity theft, have been increasing.

Majorly, Facebook has been the best platform for these criminals to employ new plans to commit crimes. To make it easier for you, my readers, let us examine this post about where you are planning to go for your holidays and are leaving for the Maldives on the very next day. Then on D Day, in a surge of extra enthusiasm, you have updated your status: 'Travelling to the Maldives for a short vacation.'

Now understand, cybercriminals actually use the same information to hawk their services and create plans that can actually be harmful to you. Even before the same, if you have kept the same information stating that your future plans are to go to the Maldives, you can find an increase of unsolicited calls, links, and messages coming from fake and fraudulent users, ultimately leaving you as a victim of cybercrimes through Facebook use.

Another important factor which has increased online interaction is that people are more involved in live streaming and video creation. Going by the above instance, the same demographics are being used by criminals to create identity thefts.

In a recent survey, it has been observed that even WhatsApp audio messages have been used to create and forge links for spreading misinformation. As I've already made evident, the fact is that WhatsApp is not private. You must be curious about this phenomenon of how these audio messages have been used to create/forge links for spreading misinformation,

You must be clear, according to the above statement, as to how these audio messages are being used. To make it clearer, let me cite an example. In a recent terrorist plant that was about to be executed in one of the states, it was being observed that the audio messages shared by the attackers were actually an illusion of a different voice.

At the same time, to decode their attacks, there were several platforms created by these attackers. So, you see that the interplay of human interaction with Social Media platforms has given rise to an emergence of complexity in such cases.

Picking another example for consideration, during the Farmers'
Protest, we had seen multiple views and comments posted by the users. The same comments and online interaction led to several attacks happening after 15 August.

If we reassess the situation we see that audiences, through the increased political journalism, as also social media platforms, were recipients of multiple perspectives through these mutual interactions and the outcomes were being well used by politicians as well as farmers. If we examine all the above situations, we will realize that we are ultimately being dragged into middle trajectories, through the mirage of online spaces of interaction.

The traditional ways of sending promises, which at one time were the passwords of Indian politics, at these elections were not seen much. It has been stated that during this period nearly one-third of first-time voters got influenced through these Social Media campaigns. A report by ADG online states that 30% of the 10 million first-time voters were influenced and were engaging more on Social Media.

So, all these online interactions, trolls, and posts, clearly state that today, to reach either the urban or the rural voters all you have to do is be significantly active on Social Media. After the winning of the BJP in 2014, a maximum number of Maharashtra regional parties became active on Social Media. Recently, BJP leaders who are involved in elections-related publicly to 'Economic Times' that the party's total advertisements expenditure accounted for 20-25% of the total budget and which were posted on these Social Media campaigns. They spent nearly Rs. 37 crores on Facebook advertisements. During the same period in question, the Congress Party had spent Rs. ten lakhs whereas regional parties had spent Rs 20 lakhs.

So Social Media platforms, for whom we were the only source of income, are today, minting money through these political parties' status updates.

Chapter 13

Atma Nirbhar Social Media

Since we have been using the well recognized Social Media Apps, Facebook, Instagram, and Twitter, I think the current government has realized the fact that the Indian market is a goldmine for these foreign Social Media Apps. The reason behind such thinking is that after the prohibition of TikTok and other Chinese Apps, the Prime Minister has urged the citizens to shift to Indian Social Media Apps, like Koo, ShareChat, Roposo, SquadCam, Elyments, and Chingari, to come into the picture.

The question is, how much have Indian markets adapted themselves through these Apps? Let us take a brief about these Indian-based Apps, starting with the ShareChat app. ShareChat App offers private messaging. This platform allows users to share social content even through to unknown users. Founders Ankush Sachdeva, Bhanu Pratap Singh, and Farid Ahsan say that their current mobile application has currently 160 million App users. Another plus point is that you can use this App of theirs in 15 different languages. Besides the above, this App also won the government's ***'Aatmanirbhar Bharat App Innovate Challenge'***.

Another App similar to the above-mentioned App is the 'Koo' App, which claims to hold the same capabilities as Twitter. Like ShareChat, it also lets users publish in Indian languages, other than Hindi. In the Koo App, a user can limit up to 400 characters of text which is a much higher figure than even Twitter.

After the banning of TikTok, many toyed with the idea of having an Indian-based video platform. That was the precise reason why the Chingari App came into the picture. Through this App, users have a choice of uploading videos in 20 Indian languages.

Yet, in spite of these innovative Apps, the dominance of foreign Apps remains the same. Even when Indian Apps have been replicas of these foreign Apps the Indian market has not completely accepted these Apps. It leads one to enquire, therefore, whether the banning of foreign Apps mentioned earlier, was necessary.

It may interest you to know that there is more than one lakh, sixty-one thousand Apps from Indian publishers on Google Play, yet still, only a few have marked their presence in the market.

Ever since the banning of foreign Apps came about, the Indian Apps that were created during that period gained popularity. You might even say that most of the Social Media Apps don't have their copies in India. But that is not the whole truth. If you are thinking of Apps like Tinder, which too, are not having their copy, then let me tell you, we do have an App that is banned, in India, called 'Flick'. It provides both the features of a Social Media App as also a dating App.

And yet the above-mentioned Apps do not carry much recognition. This is similar to the situation where you cannot expect an Indian housewife to get used to a roti maker in place of the traditional griddle. Thus, you cannot expect Indian users who are used to foreign Apps to make the same kind of rapport with Indian brands.

You might again question whether a particular App has its active users. But in reality, we see that out of the total Indian population, only one-tenth of it is using Indian brands. Personally, I'm glad that these Apps, which we launched after the ban, have got some popularity. Otherwise, Apps which were launched long before the ban would never have gained the acceptance they have, and the reason why they would have had to be removed.

The conclusion remains that these apps will only get the right acceptance once they are being promoted equally and at par, with the foreign Apps. Also, it should be strictly enforced that Indian Apps should be used. The whole influencer community, which continuously keeps promoting their content on these foreign Social Media Apps, if forced to a single contributing towards the India-grown Apps, then the usage of Facebook, Twitter, Instagram Apps, will see a decline.

Chapter 14

The Whistle Blower

I might sound a little like someone who has decided to come forward and provide you with information which can be the key to improve many lives, or someone who could be a part of these organisations who goes about disclosing information to the public. I leave the choice of decision to you, to decide who I am. Call me either, or the Hand of God.

In 1989, the ... to protect several government employees in the United States, from retaliatory action, for volunteers disclosing information about illegal activities, the Whistle Blower Protection Act had been introduced. Someone reporting the wrongdoings of a media channel was termed as a whistleblower. Since then, many such cases have come into the picture, wherein employees have decided to come forward and let us, the public, know the real identity of the organization's working.

Exactly back in November 2021, the Facebook whistleblower stated that the company that was building Metapurse, a virtual reality version of the Internet, is a dangerous platform, which could increase privacy problems. She stated that Facebook wants to occupy the space with microphones, sensors, to monitor us in all possible ways. For example, she stated that if you are working from home, and your employer decides to be a Metapurse company, then basically you give the liberty to Facebook to spy on you. In an interview she even stated clearly that this Social Media giant, entrusting vulnerable leans, in all possible ways, mentioning again, that Facebook users profit over toxic content.

For the same, Mark Zuckerberg stated that the content present on the platform is being deliberately pushed by us as illogical. The question arises, therefore, why did Mark Zuckerberg even spare his time to debate on this when he knew it was illogical? It seems in the year 2021, Facebook which reported profits of nine billion dollars, was trying to save his pocket money!

Another case happened where another whistleblower stated that Facebook-owned Instagram is far worse and more dangerous as a Social Media platform. Instagram recently introduced a filter to guide users regarding breast self-examination. Johnson and Johnson, consumer health, the world's largest healthcare company, used this special filter to provide help regarding breast self-care. Basically, the mobile display becomes a mirror where a projected animation guides the movement on the spot of the breast. They stated that through science and innovation, they wanted to let their service for women care especially.

The question arises, if this filter could actually guide us regarding self-care, they could have kept a boundary wherein the usage of the filter was not allowed to be posted on the walls of Instagram. But it seems, Johnson and Johnson, along with Instagram, were much more interested in making make this publicity stunt to be seen by the public. As accurately stated by the whistleblower, Instagram then, is about social comparison and bodies and the reason why the usage of such filters is making the scenario worse for young adults and teens.

Why an App, which specifically brings out such content, is evident in the previous last chapter. They know very well what kind of core content can drive more profit./ So it is not about self-care. It is about being self-re exposed

Even we have had cases where whistleblowers from Google too, came up to let us know regarding the scam happening inside their companies and that to hide this fact, huge amounts of money had to be spent to cover up the reality.

Hence, not just for hiding the truth, but even for trying to hide the fact about all such cases of illegal activities, remains unchecked by the Social Media giants. So, no matter how much we blow the trumpet, these Social Media giants know very well how we are being blindfolded.

Chapter 15

Algorithm, a Snowball Effect

You might be thinking that my statements are not valid because the engagement of any piece of content is because of the algorithms or Social Media platform. It is very true that all the posts that we see on the platform, abate on the kind of content we are likely to follow. So you see the pun of the situation is that the content present on the Social Media platform is because of the push it has got, by the Social Media algorithms.

To understand, let me reiterate an example. During the protest in front of Jawaharlal Nehru University, Delhi, the maximum posts that we saw were majorly about CAA, celebrities present, and against a certain community. How is it that all these instances were so much in number on the platform? The answer is very simple. There is a likelihood that the likes, comments, and shares of such posts create an increase in engagement, as there is likely to be an increase of such posts. So, you will say the matter here ends up as not being the fault of Social Media. It is 'us' who are creating such content. But the reality is, that it is not just us.

These algorithms are controversial. To understand this, for example on YouTube you can see any number of videos with millions of views. Even after your recommendation as not being interested. But still, they continue to hold the maximum number of youths. So, you see, in spite of optimizing our feed we are getting content which is not necessary. Understand that algorithms maximally show legwork for what you want, but the hidden algorithm works as a toner to increase use in the Social Media space.

It is also being believed that these algorithms also push brands and influencers to pay a premium amount to present in social ads. Frankly speaking, this is not just a statement. If you remember, it was being in the media that the Singer Badshah paid 24 lakhs for getting 72 lakh views for one of his videos. He did this in order to break a viewership record. If you don't believe it, try asking the Mumbai Police for having filed a 446-page charge sheet against him.

So, the answer is simple. That Algorithm solely does not work just based on the content which we see. It is even based on premium amounts paid by a number of celebrities and influencers.

Chapter 16

Social Media Detox

Before we plan for a holiday, stating that there would be no more mobile checking and you would be just with Nature, let me ask you, are you a hundred percent sure that you don't want to please your friends with your hashtags: Nature Live posts? I caught you on that because I am very sure that it would be difficult for you to just stay away from Social Media and its influencing community.

You might even say that the writer is back from the influencer community... that such influencers have just started growing in the past few years on the platform. But my dear friend, this personality-driven Social Media just does not have a certain number of peas in the pod. Let me hint to you that in actuality, the number is somewhere between four to 35 million in the world! So, now you tell me, how many influencers are there on Instagram, YouTube, and of course, TikTok, and how many are there, apart from these platforms?

To roughly determine the same, just fathom how many platforms you are there as an active user. I'm sure that you have landed on 3-5 platforms. In the same manner, you will find your top influencers on each platform. So, it is a kind of overlap. In the same manner, you will have individual influencers on each platform, with different user names. Hence, the overall influencer marketing ecosystem is widespread across, contributing approximately five to ten billion in the market.

It has also been noticed that Instagram alone contributes 1.5 billion dollars through the influencer community. So, both macro and micro-influencers are actually minting money by forming the hashtag: Nature's Life. This community today is occupying the space not just on the platform but also in the mindsets of the people.

It has become evident that the impact of Social Media on mental health is significant. As I have pointed out earlier, we have the maximum number of young adults getting addicted to these platforms. At the same time, it has also been observed that psychological distress is also high, among young adults. So, these digital natives are actually posing a serious concern in mental health problems.

After the release of Social media and an increase in its usage, it has been noticed that the rate of suicidal thoughts has increased during the same period. And it does not stop at the mere thought. In today's scenario, even before committing suicide, potential suicide victims let you know about the same through their status and post. The unrealistic views, peer pressure, dramatic visualization, and the lack of in-person contacts have been the major reasons for Social Media being negative.

If I have to guide you through a statistics-related data, it has been seen that between the ages of 15-17 almost 90% of teens and young adults used to own their own smartphones. Relative to an increase in the sale of smartphones is an increase by the same yardstick, among the same age group, of feelings of depression on a parallel basis. In 2017, a survey happened wherein it was found that young people from 8-12 grades had the highest level of depressive symptoms. Even the self-harm cases in the same teenager group nearly got tripled. So, you see it has only gotten worse.

The whole pattern points out that the following factors, namely the spreading of fake Images, constant asking of private images, physical threats, have affected youth from ages

18-24. At the same time, 35% of the people who have faced cyberbullying has reported mental illness. So, the approach of shared likes and re-tweets of hate, conflicts, and harassment, are the critical reasons why Social Media has negative effects. When asked of a depression facing patient as to what has hampered him the most on his path to recovery, he replied that it was an excessive trust and believing of the information on the platforms, absorbing too much sensationalism had created this mindset that he, as a person, is from out of the box. He did not feel integrated into the community.

It is important to understand that the heavy usage of being online, or rather, we can say, being readily available on social media, has uncovered negativity in an open space. So, if your child is feeling low in self-esteem and is high on anxiety, you need to sit and make him understand the real-life around him. Also, as a parent, I agree that you too, need to work upon your usage culture. Hence, every time motivating kids for self-promotion, when you all sit together for dinner and your kid, before taking a bite, stops to take a snap and keep a hashtag: Hashtag Home Food, make your kids realize that this is made of natural ingredients rather than gold. So, he should stop lime lighting each and everything.

A social media detox is necessary for getting back to living that simple life once again.

Chapter 17

They Admit

You might be under the impression that only the writer is saying that Social Media platforms are biased. But the fact is that these platforms themselves confess that they are biased. This fact was being examined when tweets from elected officials of seven different countries were taken into consideration. Twitter had admitted that they had amplified tweets from one set of politicians.

Twitter claims that its algorithm follows a chronological order. But the fact is, it amplifies as per its algorithmic timeline. It was being found that the number of users on the algorithm-tailored timeline, was much higher than that on a chronological timeline.

Twitter stated that it wasn't sure why its feed produced such results. It stated that the timeline produced preferential treatment rather than showing as per the result of the algorithm basis. It even stated that they will allow third parties to access the data and make their research, just like Facebook does. So basically, they were all clearly set to show us algorithmic transparency.

Now it comes to Facebook. Even they admitted that the misinformation is much higher on their platform. Further, Facebook also issued third parties the chance to access the data and that is the reason why we are much more aware of Cambridge Analytica. The personal data was taken by this consulting firm and the maximum number of users' information was being drained out.

Also, in a recent interview, Adam Mosseri, the head of Instagram, admitted that Facebook has a bias. He stated through a tweet that they are not neutral. It stated that they try and be apolitical but that's becoming increasingly difficult. All these statements were in the limelight when companies, including Apple, Google, Amazon, Twitter, completely banned Donald Trump from its platform. They stated that it was necessary to ban Trump from the platform as it was leading to an increase in violence in the country.

When it comes to India, many Indians lost their Blue Badge on Twitter. If you remember, the personal accounts of people like the Vice President of India, Shri Venkaiah Naidu had lost the verified Blue Badge on Twitter. When Twitter faced major outrage, it stated that this loss was due to the fact that the account had been inactive since July 2020. But when the Twitter account of RSS Chief Mohan Bhagwat lost the verified Badge, Twitter stated that it happened because of its new verification policy.

When people questioned such instances, stating that have been various other accounts which are not active for some time, then why is their verified badge still in place. For the4 same, Twitter stated that the inactivity on both the above-mentioned accounts was based on their logging in. They stated it is important actually, for the users who have verified badges, to log in at least once every six months.

After 2017, the company even suspended new verification requests on the platform. During the Farmers' Protest, it was being noticed that many accounts were being suspended based on the norm of platform manipulation and Spam. The common thing which was being seen was that the accounts that were against the Framers' Protest were suspended.

As per Twitter, it was being stated that these accounts were amplifying conversations related to violence. By that logic, the conclusion then drawn is that showing favor towards a whole lot of protest was not leading to violence, as per Twitter, but standing up against the same, was violating Twitter's rules and regulations.

In all the above scenarios you see how these platforms had failed to know their own truth.

Chapter 18

Face-Off Projects

With over 32,000 followers on Instagram, Rachita Taneja started off the Greenpeace Foundation campaign and was vocal about environmental causes. Social Media artists and influencers, as I have repeatedly been saying, are playing a major role in creating the campaign altogether.

During the protest against NRC and CAA, more than half of the nation was active through Social Media. The images floating on each and every platform created visuals that triggered reactions from many of the people. Not just Social Media alone, but the whole influencer community came as a boom, in spelling out rumors across the platform.

As I say, online activism has become the face of street protests. It may be worthwhile to recall that during the CAA and NRC protests, no political party came on the streets to explain, or rather communicate, with the people. It was just Social Media communication that was transforming every next step of the protest.

If we deep-dive into these topics, you will find that these platforms are not just organizers but also facilitators of such campaigns across the globe. Even during the 'Black Lives Matter' campaign, Instagram and Twitter came out on their platforms to advocate much more about one site, and about organizing the protest.

Coming to the Nirbhaya case also, as also among the maximum rape cases reported, you could see an ample variety of emotions floating on the platform, creating much more frenzy and an environment of hatred. You could see the stark picture in an aggressive reaction mode, from not just the common man, but also from political parties.

In the era of such media, it seems everyone has gotten access to being the broadcaster. If you still feel that that's not the truth about the above, go back to the days when the Farmers' Protest happened in India. After 11 August, it was not just we who got to see the emotions coming from Indian citizens, but also, there were mocking statements from Pakistan.

A whole lot of these reactions led to the next day's situation wherein men in uniform were being manhandled, and a series of ugly incidents took place. You could see that the whole country was divided into two. It is very true that these medians can make even a remote place issue into a global issue through its impact.

Even going back to the days when Anna Hazare had started off with his campaign, we could see the country getting united against corruption. Smelling the impact, platforms are maturing, and much more of such events can be expected to be coming into reality, in the forthcoming days. We are very sure that after a couple of years, India would be standing as a Supreme Power but to make this possible we need to stop believing the impact disseminated out by these platforms.

Chapter 19

Digital Health

Let me give you the top seven Social Media acquisitions that have created history. Yahoo purchased Tumblr for $1.1 billion. The strategic move made by its CEO Marissa Mayer was to bring Yahoo to speed, up to Social. At that time, the purchase seemed to be a good move. But as Tumblr's traffic started stagnating, Yahoo faced a major challenge.

The very next acquisition that brought dynamic change was when Microsoft bought Yammer, in 2012. Microsoft stated that Yammer would be integrated with Microsoft Office Division. The idea was to increase productivity through various software and services.

Way back in June 2013, Twitter decided to buy Wine that tracked at the cost of $970 million, when Twitter was just subjected to a certain set of characters. This acquisition defined various parameters. Twitter's acquisition of 'Wine' turned into an interesting deal, where Wine's six-second videos used to go hand-in-hand with Twitter's 140 characters.

When Israeli start-up Waze Mobile, was purchased by Google, everyone wondered why a company like Google had bought this start-up and that too, at the cost of $966 million. This acquisition was basically done because Google wanted to stand out of its competition by building a community, through localized mapping and routing.

The very next acquisition which we are well aware of is Facebook buying WhatsApp and Instagram, at the cost of $19 billion and $ One billion, respectively. We are very much aware of the fact that after this acquisition both WhatsApp and Instagram got the maximum number of users in comparison to what they had had earlier. A fourth article states that when Facebook bought Instagram, Facebook itself bought over thirty million 'Tipsters'.

Coming to the next purchase, a much older one, but still, a sensational acquisition was the one when Google bought YouTube, at the cost of $1.65 billion. The purchase was not just used for Google history but also for the fact that it gave Google another marketing arm.

Why I have been discussing these purchases and acquisitions is to help you understand that dominance by these platforms is increasing. Somebody had rightly stated that if something is free, then you are the product. This is not a complaint but an observation to let you understand that these companies, which are the world's most successful business giants, have revenues across a million companies.

To cite an example, a company like Apple has a revenue of $ 3 million; Facebook has a revenue of $3.70 lakhs, and Google across $ one million. The same is the case with Microsoft. Lydon Solutions has a revenue of approximately $ 55,000; Netflix has a revenue of around $ one lakh, while Twitter has a revenue of approximately $ 50K.

I would request you to read the revenues again and again and take note of the fact that these numbers are increasing every second because we, as products are embracing them with our information. We need to understand that by optimizing the cost and the content, they are developing better strategies.

The information reveals that these companies are run by tech-savvy millenniums and Gen-Z. It has even been estimated that the advertising market for free advertisement-supported video services, is to double in the next two years.

So, the gateway of content supplied by us is booming, with about a quarter of different services being commanded by

Social Media services. So, it is necessary to control the content-generating, and stabilize the feeds, to ensure that the world does not become just a stage.

The Final Destination

The feeling of being one of a community always allows one to create an atmosphere where you can learn more. Sharing information, ideas, and common interests, makes it far easier for us to develop and navigate with information. But it is rightly stated that too much of anything creates a lot of negative effects. Throughout this journey the 'funda' was to let you understand that the basic goal of these social media platforms was to allow us to communicate.

Because of the depletion of face-to-face interactions Social Media came in as a medium for us. But at the same time, it has, in recent times, been impacting us in so powerful a manner that we are getting deprived of real-life skills due to it. The blue tick mark or the hashtag, or the re-tweets has been made as slaves of these platforms. Besides, our getting overly engulfed in this virtual world, is also impacting all of society.

I remember when I was facing psychological depression my psychologist asked me to interact more with Nature and avoid the virtual world. She clearly stated that since I had got stuck in these virtual dimensions, I had lost the connection with Mother Nature. At the same time, I remember those days too, when as a teenager, my parents used to ask me to give time to what was happening, rather than putting in effort towards building Social Media profiles.

Frankly speaking, even I belong to the same community, at the same time, I've understood how these 'likes' and 'forwards' have impacted real life. I again reiterate that I'm not asking you to just get rid of the thing because even I understand that to move along with today's fast forward lifestyle their presence is important.

But just the presence, as compared to a permanent relationship, is far different. You can remove the traces but just cannot get them out of your path. Hence, just keep Social Media platforms as traces. Do not hold on to them as permanent relationships.

Your every decision impact and affects the environment. And getting influenced by this limelight-driven world has just made you forget how to create a self-image. If you and I together push for a regulatory impact, for these platforms I'm sure even the online spaces will become a happy world.

Obviously, it is not that easy to bring things under control, but at the same time, our full intervention towards our usage can create positive outlines for our daily basis. So keep the technology just as a medium. Do not deflect the medium to intrude and influence your private spaces.

In short, you can be a source of information but do not become a freebie for these platforms. Not everything requires for it to be a part of when you celebrate the moment in your life; so do not ask your mobile phone to be a part of the same.

Breathe in the natural air rather than smelling the vibrations of the forwards. I'm pretty much sure that the dismantling approach carried out by these 'likes' and 'forwards' and re-tweets will not propagate after you have flipped through the pages of this book. But if it still continues to influence your life then I can only congratulate you for getting trapped by automated realities.

It is therefore your call to live a life or to live a robotic life.

9 789354 725111

Printed by Libri Plureos GmbH in Hamburg,
Germany